Life's Shadows

Also by Barbara Gurney and published by Ginninderra Press
Footprints of a Stranger

Barbara Gurney

Life's Shadows

Life's Shadows
ISBN 978 1 74027 940 6
Copyright © text Barbara Gurney 2015
Cover: Alison Mutton

First published 2015 by
GINNINDERRA PRESS
PO Box 3461 Port Adelaide SA 5015
www.ginninderrapress.com.au

Contents

Sing Loudly	7
Waiting	8
Do you see me?	9
Old Enough for War	10
Accountable	12
us	14
between	15
Krásney Neznámy	16
Sometimes Life Gets in the Way	18
Beyond	19
Ruby's with the Angels	20
Little Bird	21
The Outstretched Hand	22
They Came By Sea	23
Scatter	24
Sharna	25
Meeka	26
Morning Stroll	27
Be Gone	28
We Continue…	29
If	30
I Do	31
Broken	32
Conquering	33
Today I Smiled	34
Someone Else	35
Summer Sunset	36
The Ticket Home	37
Book of Poems	38
Purpose	39

Stealth	40
The Child	41
Haiyan	42
High Tea	43
Survival	44
Connection	45
Alone	46
The Fallow Tomb	47
Friend	48
Violin	49
Time Given	50
Plains of Lebanon	51
Daggers of Language	52
Internal Seasons	53
Forever?	54
Angels	55
Rejected Proposal	56
Menu	57
discarded	58
Final Calm	59

Sing Loudly

Life is to grow
Not to dally amid grumblers
Or listen to rumour
For days are better spent

Dishes neatly stacked
Floor duly swept
Give less pleasure than walking a dog

To sip from the cup served by a friend
Describes caring without any words

Paddle in cool water
When stress overtakes your calm

Dance with a lover
Skip with a child

Wander through bush heralding new growth
Pass by the lizard enjoying the sun
Inhale soft-scented air
Whistle with birds
Lest you forget they are there

Open your heart
Sing loudly

Waiting

Autumn leaves disintegrate on the damp ground of winter

Long shadows of sorrow fall across my shoulders
Loneliness stifles like a heavy coat on a day full of sunshine

Maybe a summer smile will appear on your face and speak to my cold heart

Do you see me?

Do you see me
With sightless vision
Beyond the statute of identity
To the pulse of truth
Where I feel
Where I am

Dreams long held
Sent into salty tears
Reflected in a smashed mirror of hope
Brittle and exposed

I'm there
Desires hoarded in a money box of longing

Reach under my facade
Delve into the depths
Where I feel
Where I am

Old Enough for War

He is only thirteen
But old enough for war

He's seen things that no one should see

Missiles screech, echoing historic battles
People huddle against insanity
Desiring the peace stolen so long ago
Wanting calm, fearing final obliteration

Angry memories tucked in corners
Too many coffins in stony graves
Lives lost for holy sacrifice
Directed from golden palaces

In a collision of cultural calamity
Scattered foe lies unidentified
Souls surrender against living
With the birthright of war

Roots of trees face the sun
Buildings imitate skeletons
Water flows from exploded pipes
Washing dreams, leaving dirty feet

Sparks fly from overhead wires
While the school mimics midnight
Desks upturned by fright
Learning scattered by horror

Families cower against yesterday's obscenities
Scrawny babies, unable to cry
Wounds sprinkled on old people
And a dog with three legs, running

No one issued him a uniform
Just gave him a gun
Told him to fight
Beyond the reality of defending

When friends were blown to smithereens
He wished angels were real
But when blood flowed from his veins
He wanted his god to be true

He'd seen things that no one should see

He was only thirteen
But old enough for war

Accountable

Colours of aspiration
      orange of optimism
      green of growth
      blue: peace and respect

Why do we choose grey
      of indecision
           of compromise

bound in lost integrity
      filtered by the world
           through uncommitted critics

hesitant to stand
      against error
           of questionable demands

Then to do nothing!

You cannot
      own ignorance
           from an exposed message

lessons without obligation
      inadequate!

pain once learnt
      custody belongs

Don't question
      the capacity within
Don't doubt
      the potency of one

Build on fervour
    reflect the spectrum of all colours

Where the message
    is vibrant
        meaningful

Where knowledge
    is accountable

us

there was you
wanting me to stay
offering your strength
to bite my shame
spit it out into colourful memories
design a new beginning
create a building block of happiness

there was me
thinking I should go
disgraced by my choices
huddled in my past
a monochrome of solitude
unable to take
not willing to give

so I left
took humiliation with me
wrapping it around lost dreams

birth

death

to survive the distance / between / one must have hope

Krásneý Neznámý

(Beautiful Stranger)

His nose lay on the footpath
Both coloured grey
Strong eyes reached mine
I stepped slowly
Wanting to touch

His man was just beyond
Across the road
Buying cigarettes
To puff away the time
Talking to rid the silence

The mat was thick brown hessian
Not washed but without a tear
The folds clearly visible
Carefully placed
Near protective trees

The sun was strong
Between the leaves
Scattered on fading brown
Dancing on this Shepherd's coat
Well lived

He stood up and shook
Lapped cool water from a cut off bottle
Licked his mouth and hesitated
Then he took two steps
Towards me
I spoke in foreign mutterings
Translation not required
But in that moment a bond
Of wanting
For both

I often chose that busy street
Sometimes inconvenient
Treading alternative cobblestones
Between home and chore
Beyond the quick

But I wanted to know
He was safe another day
That nothing changed
His contentment remaining
Always there

I left him near the gutter
Other shoes to watch
While I travelled away
With him in my memory
Never forgotten

Sometimes Life Gets in the Way

Between waking and rest
Nature's splendour snubbed in haste
        Overlooked

Morning dew falls on unseen beauty
A newborn rose ruptures without applause
        Ignored

A loved one welcomed in keystrokes
Friendship touted only by technology
        Inferred

As the air softens into glorious evening
We hurry to view someone else's dream
        Indifferent

Beyond

My eyes see someone familiar
Your face creates confusion
My cheek accepts the kiss
But I struggle with the reality of knowing

Shadows are covering my mind
Recognition is smothered by distortion

I can almost touch the past
It wanders
Then jolts
Trickles beyond recall
Beyond invisible boundaries
Leaving behind tears
And heartache without knowledge of why

Remember me
because
I cannot remember you

Ruby's with the Angels

I longed for her, to hold her tight
But all came to nothing that fateful night
The pain and anguish can't be undone
So wrap your wings around my precious one

Whisper my words she cannot hear
Tenderly wash Ruby with my tears
Tell her my love is sent in a prayer
Grant her a morrow that I cannot share

Tell her pink booties and her teddy still lay
In her cot; although she never will play
Make sure she knows of the special star
That reflects my love, ever so far

Make her understand that I'm always near
Give her my love and make it clear
She'll be my daughter; never denied
Tucked in my heart, as if by my side

Little Bird

Dance on little bird
Treat me with your joy

Share your pleasant story
Let me know your true delight

He flies
And swoops
Darting amongst the blossoms

I smile
And laugh
Content with this happy moment

The Outstretched Hand

Is society so eager to outstretch its hand

Not offering a touch of friendship
But grasping opportunity of self-benefit
Seeing others as a vessel of desires
Coveting even that which isn't needed

Taking with gluttony and avarice
        – I want
        – must have

Has greed reduced us to begging without need?
Not seeing those whose hunger is real
        – barefooted and homeless

Is it Me first, and You only if excess is superfluous?
Indifferent but for the bubble of self
Uncaring but for acquisition

The fires of society burn out of control
        – scavenging
        – looting

Because of the habit of using others

They Came By Sea

Tears washed uncompromisingly by the sea
Swallowing bodies
Pushing against flaying arms

A touch could be a friend
Name unknown

Endless waiting in salty mire
Throats longing for water
Wrinkled skin begging for relief
Wanting freedom from dread
Breathless terror surrounded by diminishing screams

Moonlight shines on struggling flotsam
The upturned hull of promises
Hope floats beyond reach
Sinking to depths of unwritten stories

2012: another refugee boat sinks

Scatter

One's life
Mimicking an upturned jigsaw
No sense in its confusion

Edges pushed into shape
Like a day without choice
Colours demand attachment
To build the anticipated story

Does life have only one path
Each piece fitting where it should
To the sameness
No matter the hand that touches

No allowance for variation
No alteration or modification
Only obligation for completion

Scatter them
Toss each piece from its prediction
Create challenge
Experience change
With a taste of determination
A smell of victory

Sharna

Her agony isn't pain
She's beyond the torture of ailments
Claimed by the daze of weakness
In the clutch of a creeping menace

Paws of gaiety long gone
The joy of running ceased
The smile of her tail stands still
While the shine in her eye has clouded

Unable to bear our hand
Her life slipped slowly away
Beyond the carefree days
And glittering diamond memories

       But there is pain –

Strangling our hearts
With torment of absence
Gripping the hunger of yearning
For that spot on the chair to be filled

An ache for the softest touch
Of the head turned on the shoulder
For the silence of her being
And the happiness of her greeting

       Farewell Tippy-toes

March 2012: the loss of our beloved Sharna

Meeka

Suddenly with strangled breath
Her eyes begging for mercy
Fear; a companion

She gave so much
Joy announced by her tail
Laughter in her soul

Our Meeka

So willing to do
So eager to be

Ever remembered

Our Meeka

June 2012: the loss of our beautiful Meeka

Morning Stroll

Shimmering strands of the morning snail
Amid mulch of yesterday's life
Crunching stones move beneath my feet
The smell of brushed peppermints linger
Gentle rain mingles with sweat
Birds join my day with beating wings
I move beyond their fear
Softness of nature enfolds the view
Drooping branches ache with springtime glory
Peeking sunshine brings anticipation
The day welcomes me

Be Gone

Don't touch my heart right now
It's fragile
With crystallised fragments
Shuddering
Ready to evaporate
Beyond nothing

Avoid my eyes
Or you'll see terror
Torn shreds of history
Refusing a future

Lay no finger on my skin
It crawls under delusion
Of tenderness

Tick, tock

Abscond from my person
As time beats its fury

Tick, tock

Freedom beckons

Leave

Leave

We Continue…

Trees obliterated by society
Flora uprooted for an unconcerned populace
Stubbled ground cleared by unsympathetic authority

No protests
Over one small acre
Why care?

       but…

A bobtail's home
Not harming
Just being
For immeasurable time

       now…

Pattering over hot bitumen
Away from noise; in terror
A refugee from destruction
Scurrying for cover
Amid superficial borders
Trimmed edges
Cultivated roses

He can't go back

       and yet…
       we continue…

If

If I was someone else
Not hurt by my life

If memories – dissolved

If I could reach beyond self-imposed limitations

Learning, trusting

If fear was gone

I Do

Uniting the future
        with passion
        of promise

Reach to the heart of two rings
        blessed with a union
        eternal

Broken

He stood
Remembering broken promises
Shattered
Like the hammer at his feet

Claws of steel
Cold as a meaningless embrace
Splintered handle
Fragmented

But one needing the other

Conquering

I sink beneath the waves
Disregard thoughts of survival

Air-filled bubbles ooze from me
Each reaching for the blue of the sky
Where clouds drift
Like me

The caress of the sea
Scolds me with cold
Embraces, then threatens
Touches my thoughts of oblivion

Inevitability seeps into each pore
Gently accepting without question
This watery grave
Tosses aside consequences
It lets me be

I claim this moment
To stay beyond reality
Possess solitude
A moment of liberty

The sun shivers across the surface
Peeks through the azure
Smiles without assurances
Promises a tomorrow

I surface and gasp at life

Today I Smiled

There's no reason for this smile

Just to while away the time in idle miles of happy thoughts

Denying the trials of yesterday with wakeful dreams of increasing joy

Someone Else

Trembling hands seek refuge
Desirous of stillness
Reaching for the beauty of gentle touch

A tongue of rock
Searches for speech
Restless lips release only unwanted noise

I used to dance
…sing

Summer Sunset

I remember the summer sunset
Beauty enveloping us
Bodies sensually tangled
As soft rays created silhouettes
With waves mellowing over our feet

We sank
Not only in soft salty sand
Deep into emotion
Of togetherness
Highlighted by the summer sunset

Turned from the finishing picture
The touch of immodest lips
Lingering like a summer sunset
Burning an eternal message
To promised hearts

Nocturnal breezes whispered
Wrapping us closer
Blending lengthening shadows
Making the night belong
Pledging the summer sunset

The Ticket Home

Journeys over, or just beginning
Bags packed with anticipation, now shattered
The slaughter of innocent travellers
Their destination unreached

An iPad blasted mid-game
Blown apart by sky-bound terror
Belongings lay tumbled and dirtied
Souvenirs broken and buried

Disputed fields collide with outrage
Faceless radicals refuse tenure
Bodies guarded, plundered
Guns readied, compassion denied

Families grieving for reason
Waiting with heartbreak
There's blood on the ticket home
And no one knows why

Flight MH17, Eastern Ukraine, 17 July 2014

Book of Poems

pages of illusions
peeking into the subconscious

Pages written
Pages typed
Pages printed
Pages turned

precious outpourings
imprinted across memories

Purpose

The waves slam towards resolution
hitting the shore with persistence
sucked into depths unfathomable

Slanting colours of the departing sun
sprayed by salty rainbows
accentuating lace-top crests and seaweed-coloured shallows

the day is ending

        but…

the ebb and flow is unrelenting

tossing waters continue
eating up sand
breaking across footprints
clearing the way for tomorrow

Stealth

Independence steals from the heart
the joy of being needed

Teach them
Let them go
Leaving all but the grip of love

Remnants of yesterdays
Imbedded memories
lingering
despite separation

Independence gives the heart
the joy of being needed

The Child

I felt crushed by pain as they entered the chapel
Strong arms weak with grief
Carrying a small white casket
Decorated with despair

Many wept
Sorrow strangled lives
Gripped with unwelcome connection

Music of soft heartache clung to the rafters
Then another sound hovered
Caused me to pause
Made me turn

A movement of air
The resonance of a spirit
Caressing the bereaved

It sounded like angels crying as they spread their wings to receive the child

Haiyan

Cruel winds fling everything from its path

Shattered houses sprinkled across the landscape
— like condiments

Grief not yet claimed
Shock hovering
— waiting to land

A huddle of children cling under a sheet of tin
A flapping tent
— a luxury

And when the typhoon stops…
heartbreak stays

Malaysian typhoon, November 2013

High Tea

I see lipstick on smiles
Painted toes peeking from stilettos
There's clinking of tea cups
And nibbling on strawberries
Dresses of pale pink and turquoise
A warm welcome for those met before
Instant connection with a new found friend

    Look closely

    Listen carefully

Purposeful conversation encompasses the room
There's determination in questions
Positivity in answers
Agreement through debate
A sharing of objectives

Heed the women with steel in their eyes

Survival

Five thousand brumbies gallop to excess
The ancient plains battle to cope
Summer edges of billabongs crumble
And winter mud is disturbed by hooves

The wattle and the ghostly gums
Bend under advancing global warming
The corroboree frog fights for its home
It's the emblem of the struggle

Human bickering threatens the peaceful hills
Guns offered in solutions name
No solace for the mighty stallions
The brumbies of the Mount

Debate is strong, the pull for equal ground
The earth must surely be sustained
The brumbies and the little frog
Need Kosciuszko to survive

Connection

I walked beside a child
She skipped
               … I didn't

We stopped
She smiled
Held out her hand
               … We skipped together

Alone

I sit enveloped by emotion
    Ignored
    Insignificant
    Invisible

Filling the space and not the heart

Demands are met and honestly given
    But where is the caring for the one alone?

Is my presence useful
    But only for the time set aside for our encounter?

Is this my lot?
    To be alone
    Surrounded by the world

The Fallow Tomb

The clock ticks

but…

        will it be silenced
        will there be no tomorrow

Imagine nothing
An earth exploded into bleakness
Particles of yesterdays
Blood red in isolated drifts of ash
Floating, drifting
Odour of desolation and grief
Clinging to a dreamless void

but…

        the clock continues to tick
        there is hope

Friend

Cry on my shoulder
Let me wrap your hurt in caring
Grip my hand
Hide amongst my strength

Come to me

Cry on my shoulder
Enfold your burden with tenderness
Cling to me
Take my love unto your self

Violin

I hear the violin
Embracing harmony
That settles within
Long after the strings are broken

                The cymbals
                Loud and angry
                Disappear beyond their echo

I hear the violin
Bring tears to those of learning
Bending impossible notes
Unless found in dreams

                Oboe
                Haunting sounds
                Fading like moonlight

I hear the violin
Breathless in adoration
My feet are moved to stand
The music is of hearts expanding

Time Given

Then

the thrill of waves tumbling, tossing like
    bountiful benefactors
grains forced between mellowed toes
shivering at sunrise
after long nights of empty glasses
countless days with boundless energy
scouring lanes in foreign places
reaching heights of passion
with no intention

Now

solitary days of quiet blessings
memories wrapped like a rug around aged bones
gentle passing of shared moments
left in reminiscence

possess forever the tide of life
ebbing between experiences
grieve not on regret
sit well into time given

Plains of Lebanon

A bitter land
Where the sun beats forever
Tiptoeing lizards pant their journey
Human footprints distorted, then gone
Scorched winds toss tent corners
Where the burden for man is survival

2014: The exodus from Syria

Daggers of Language

One's soul
   – defeated

by careless words

bleeding from the psyche

crushed and battered
like eggshell underfoot

Sometimes
        there's succour in silence

Internal Seasons

Drip with the sunshine of joy
And a velvet voice of pleasure
See beyond the commonplace
With the heat of enthusiasm

Loosen the hurt of the past
From the boundary of doubt
Experience the vibrancy of change
With colours of inspiration

Rain gently with retrospection
Reach beyond the storms
Feed the soul with contentment
Smatter your journey with love

Find within, the essence of you
Embrace satisfaction
Release the energy of renewal
Take hold of the power to fly

Forever?

Why not for a moment in time
With the breath of pleasure
In a whisper of lust

Sweet memories to linger
With passing years
Without regret

Shared beyond love
In a moment of time

Angels

Myriad of faces
With miserable frowns
Stay bound in sadness
Of their work
Of their greed

No thoughts of joy
The merest of pleasures
Not greeting the wonder
Of the sunshine
Of the rain

Shrugging indifference
Rejecting closeness
Exposing self-interest
Of their own
Of their choice

The lightest of touch
By a finger of bliss
Would alter this gloom
Of the day
Of the hour

Angels can't fly if nobody smiles

Rejected Proposal

Sweet aroma reaches beyond my touch
Red petals
Blinding expectations
Tossed high with emotion
Fluttering down
To feet of disappointment
Dewdrops of the morning
Replaced by tears

Menu

Slavia Café
Under the shadow of a muse
Emptied bottles of discontent
Lie with solemn dogs
At the feet of unwritten passions

Imperial Hotel
Evil boots tread across memories
Shivers of recall amid beauty
Glimpses of uniforms, guns, misery…
On the underbelly of enjoyment

Kavarna Café
Opulence drips from chandeliers
Coffee soothes the traveller's cares
Yet beggars of old could only peek
Through misty windows and wonder

As one sips thick dark coffee from tiny cups, the history of these exquisite Czech buildings changes one's mood.

discarded

weeds stand tall
amid crumbling granite headstones

sunken earth
under scattered stones

faded plastic petals
of distant emotions

are we just a memory
ceasing when no one cares

lost beyond knowledge
when lineage ends

Final Calm

Essence of pleasure
Like waves caressing the sand
Bubbling on contact
An ecstasy to share
Sighing on retreat
Content with the final calm

www.ingramcontent.com/pod-product-compliance
Lightning Source LLC
Chambersburg PA
CBHW062202100526
44589CB00014B/1922